Mindscapes

POEMS BY

Lee Woodman

Winner of the 2020 William Meredith Award in Poetry

Poets' Choice Publishing

Poets-Choice.com
337 Kitemaug Road
Uncasville, Ct. 06382
MarathonFilm@gmail.com

llustrations © by Charles W. Reyburn
Cover art: "Across Fishers to Plum Island," oil on canvas, 16" x 20"
Author's photo by Sonya Melescu
Artist's photo by Patricia Reyburn
Richard Harteis photo by Michael C. Doyle
Layout by Barbara Shaw

Copyright © 2020 Poets' Choice Publishing
All Rights Reserved
Published in the United States of America

Library of Congress Cataloging-in-Publication Pending

ISBN: 978-1-7335400-4-9

Poets' Choice Publishing
Poets-Choice.com
337 Kitemaug Road
Uncasville, Ct. 06382
MarathonFilm@gmail.com

For my parents, EVERETT AND RUTH WOODMAN,
who are no longer with us, but started it all.
He told me stories of Fillilulu birds
that flew backwards,
and she taught me how to perform
boundless pirouettes

Table of Contents

Introduction vii
My Dinner with Athena 1
Blue Torso Lady 4
Victorian Ghost 6
Hymn for Emily 8
Spirits 9
It Just Won't Work 11
Pushing up Sod 12
Orchid 14
Chocolate Crescendos 15
Open Air Massage at Big Sur 17
White Lies 18
Secrets I Tell Myself 20
Seashell Symphony 21
Laila's Brain 23
Adrenaline Dog 25
Dragon Rat Nightmare 26
Wretched 28
That Sweet Dirty Smell of Children 29
A Child Asks 30
Yellow into Yellow 32
Rebirth on the Metro Quay 33
Reconsidering the Moon 34
Sorrow 36
A Life Unravels with the Day 38
In Which I Consider Myself A Possible Woman of Algiers 40
The Underside of Color 44
Story Tower 46
What to Expect at Congressional Cemetery 48
Longings 50
Cento: The Self, The Soul, The Body 52
Strange Currency 53
Mindscapes 54

Acknowledgments 56
Thanks 57
List of Paintings 58
About the Art 59
About the Author 60
Author's Statement 61

Introduction

By Richard Harteis

In a comment written for MINDSCAPES, Maryland Poet Laureate and legendary-poetry-talk-show host, Grace Cavalieri "announces a bright new literary light among us." One recalls the famous letter of Emerson to Walt Whitman who writes, "I greet you at the beginning of a great career, which yet must have had a long foreground somewhere, for such a start... It has the best merits, namely, of fortifying and encouraging." In Josephine Jacobsen's poem "Gentle Reader," she describes the experience of reading a poet, "dangerous and steep," late at night: "O God, it peels me, juices me like a press; ..... saying like Molly, yes, yes, yes O yes."

It may be gilding the lily, but Lee Woodman's poems do indeed seem at once accessible and profound and one can only wonder about the "foreground" Emerson speculates on. She seems to have arrived, full-grown like Athena from the brain of Zeus, though I'm not sure what she would make of the metaphor. This is one beautiful woman whose poems capture what it means to be female with extraordinary insight whether it be the simple grief of a mother bird who has lost a chick, to the Jungian archetype of a woman coming from the sea ("Blue Torso Lady.) In her poem, "My dinner with Athena," the goddess instructs her to "do magnificent deeds." At times the poems are nothing less.

When I first began considering Lee Woodman's poetry—and it was a unique experience for me to be publishing the work of someone I had never met—I constantly mistakenly called the manuscript DREAMSCAPES. The poems so often had the reality of dreams, that for a while, I did not even notice the mistake. "Adrenaline Dog," for example, is almost a literal translation of the anxiety one feels in dream sometimes. (I think of the Meredith's description of Trelawney, "though I am still a strong swimmer, I can feel this channel widen as I swim.") Elsewhere, she conjures Mary Queen of Scots, "Conversing with former revenants, / through language no one can hear." Lee hears it.

In his beautiful artist's statement, Charles Reyburn describes his paintings as "glimpses in which we are feeling the present-into-the future or are taken into feeling our past. A painting by hand (and mind) puts you there."

I was struck by the role the mind plays in the artist's talent. Paintings and poetry really a do have the same source which is the mind. The brain, after all, is what finally determines reality from the sensory input it receives all along the neurological line. The brain determines what is painful or beautiful. And so the title MINDSCAPES seems appropriate.

How we see, the decisions we make—blue here changes red there—are all a function of the mind. Each artist creates visions of the world using paint or words, but it is the mind that selects what is to be laid down on the canvas or blank page.

And yet there is another element as well in such landscapes/mindscapes. The artist is more than a stenographer. He intuits the ideal which infuses his work beyond the shadows seen in Plato's cave. The artist is always on guard, hoping to intuit real reality. As Meredith says in a poem, "The mind waiting for snow is the true mind."

An interviewer asked William once where he believed poetry came from and the answer, as I recall, was, God. It is certainly a mysterious event when it happens. And, if metaphor is the little engine driving poetry, love is the fuel which drives that engine. Divine or no, love is the groundwork for the visual or verbal arts. And its origin is mysterious.

A careful look at two poems reveal the "wit and wisdom" that infuses Woodman's poetry as well as the compassion found in a bodhisattva for the suffering of mankind. Her eye does not shy away from the terrifying. In "Laila's Brain," Woodman carefully traces the life of an immigrant wife and an abusive husband with the same powerful horror found in Frost's "Vanishing Red." After a mysterious car accident leaves Laila demented, she continues to rail at her dead husband on the phone, though "no one is on the line." Woodman captures the detail of this tragedy with the precision of a master detective or dramatic monologist.

In her "Hymn for Emily," Woodman hears echoes of Keats' "Ode on a Grecian Urn," and the famous last line, 'Beauty is truth, truth beauty'— that is all / Ye know on earth, and all ye need to know."

In Woodman's Hymn, she says Dickinson died for beauty:

> *I died for Beauty,* so she said
> when *Truth* lay by her side.
> So hard to picture both of them
> conversing when they died.
>
> Adjoining rooms with walls between
> kept the pair from touching.

> One had the sense despite the scene
> they really should be kissing.

Like the lovers on the urn she imagines the beauty of time and of the finite, since the lovers painted on the urn will never embrace; they are paused, about to touch each other, forever. But in Woodman's poem, Emily accepts the eternal separation:

> The tombs were still, not far apart,
> she always kept her distance.
> She must have willed thick moss to creep—
> her own passive resistance.

Lee Woodman's poems are far from only philosophical—there are the real shadows that intrigue us. "Orchid" is one of the most erotic poems I can remember. I recall Danny Abse telling me once a comment from his anatomy professor that troubled him the rest of his life: "The vagina is a potential space."

What to make of a poem like "Orchid?" How can one forget the lines:

> I arch my back on
> silken sheets.
> His breath is slow,
> there is only endless time.
> Warm fingers travel
> the arch, nuzzling over
> creamy hill and
> strawberry nipple,
> trailing downward
> to softening petals below."

Wow. I'll let it up to the reader to find his or her favorite lines. For now, Poets's Choice must thank Grace Cavalileri, our Meredith Board Member for introducing us to this "new literary light" for whom we offer the William Meredith Award for Poetry 2020 with such pleasure and gratitude.

Richard Harteis, Foundation President, inscribing his recently published collection of poems, *Mystical Rehab*.

My Dinner with Athena

She enters in gossamer white, aqua shawl
A huge golden pendant resembling an owl

She lays down her sword, puts it under the table
Tosses her ringlets, fingers her sable

I start with some questions, she stops to confer
Can our waiter bring sea bass with olives for her?

He nods yes of course, his voice very low
Says our wine is divine, we should try Orvieto

Interrupted by flagrant toasts to her gardens,
And then by her boasts of sculptures, tall fountains

I start to forget why I wanted a mentor
She blithely neglects the reason we met here

So, I endure long tales of her party,
Held in plein air, right next to the priory

Barbequed lamb, golden flames burning brightly
Her fans all brought gifts, they know she's quite arty

She relished the game of putting that guy down
The one with the cloak, sharp trident upturned

Both were aware of their upcoming skirmish
Wily and fearless, she knew she would vanquish

I stop her mid-story, as I scream, "Athena!
I need you to focus! Pay attention to me—

Tell me how did we get here? Pray, what do you know?"
She takes a small sip, hazel eyes start to glow—

Then she chants:
Life is dangerous, thrilling and glorious
Work hard in your fields, don't make it laborious

Spin marvelous magic, be tough and ambitious
Keep reading, keep reading, be slyly capricious

Help all of your babies, give parties for friends
Do magnificent deeds!

And that was the end

She never explained the way we all got here
She was late for a séance, and readied to go

Floated up to the spot where her entourage waited
Climbed into the carriage and wrote on a scroll

I think she recorded a thought from our meeting
Silver ink— perhaps it was something I said?

She waved from her chariot, looking resplendent
Murmured a blessing—personal, transcendent:

May the gods be with you!

Daffodils & Small Waterfall, 9 x 12, oil on canvas

Blue Torso Lady

Long-legged creature, translucent blue torso, stands at the shore
wondering

Sandpipers swoop forward peeping, skittering. Darting in lockstep,
they make quick reverses, greedily dipping long beaks for eggs

Beguiled, she scans the unending horizon, ears catching echoes
of gulls forming V's

She sways with acres of sapphire waves that dance the diagonal,
turning to cobalt

A following wind blows whispers to whitecaps, she lifts her own
shoulders high for a breath

The furl advances nearer, steeper 'til crests topple over,
crystals fly skyward

Blue torso lady breathes the sharp fragrance, salt droplets fall on her
nose, lips, and eyelids

She lunges forward, dives into the whorl, she knows how to spiral,
loop round the curl

Billows of breakers churn at the surface, creatures respond by circling
below Long-legged lady is whirling mid starlight,

swimming in concert with luminous squid. She'll stay there forever,
breathing is easy. At depth she can swallow, she's seahorse and brine

All at once the moon pulls and turns the sea calmer, waves
slide forth sidesaddle, sitting on time

Gently they spill frilly arcs up the beachfront,
large sprays of seaweed drop inkblots on shore

Destined, she is drawn to the coastline. Before long,
pulled from the water toward dunes

To-and-fro swash is chased by shore pipers,
low-flying birds cry out her name

Wisps of green hair swish around pebbles,
foamy blue bubbles roll over sand

Something has ended where it began—
No one told her she came from the sea

Victorian Ghost

Relating back to Pomfret Castle,

she conjures Henry's Catherine

and Mary, Queen of Scots, as she wanders

through walls in diaphanous white—

a collar of broderie anglaise holds up her neck,

a ruffled yoke covers her breast.

Shell buttons crawl down her sleeves

toward lacy cuffs

that hide the secret of her wrists.

Conversing with former revenants,

through language no one can hear,

she learns of left-behind diaries,

stark warnings, invisible ink.

Mostly she prefers to glide around the tower,

passing through light shafts, staring at mirrors.

At times she'll brush her toe along the bronze ring

chained to the floor, luring disaster.

She's heard the guards whisper, "Oubliette, Oubliette."

She knows it's a quick slide down the ancient chute.

Nehantic Park, 16 x 20, oil on canvas

Hymn for Emily

—after Emily Dickinson's I Died for Beauty

I died for Beauty, so she said
when *Truth* lay by her side.
So hard to picture both of them
conversing when they died.

Adjoining rooms with walls between
kept the pair from touching.
One had the sense despite the scene
they really should be kissing.

The tombs were still, not far apart,
she always kept her distance.
She must have willed thick moss to creep—
her own passive resistance.

Spirits

Call me Hecate, I travel by night,
my broom casting spells upon men.
They wonder why I must take flight.

Compare me to fleet Aphrodite,
crooning love songs as she ascends.
Call me Hecate, I travel by night

to conjure new schemes I raise to incite,
aware that the change I require offends,
small wonder that I must take flight.

Antigone warns by sharing foresight
how women can stand unrepentant.
Call me Hecate, I travel by night.

Explore, rebel! To create is my right.
I need warriors, noble gents to attend,
not wonder why I must take flight.

Harken the wild man, the lover and knight
who pushes me higher, delights in my pen.
Call me Hecate, I travel by night, as
darkness descends I bloom and take flight.

Looking Down into North Adams, 16 x 12, oil on canvas panel

It Just Won't Work

> *—inspired by Hans Christian Andersen's* fairy tale,
> "Thumbelina"

A female one-third of an inch tall
will never live underground well.

She sleeps in a walnut shell,
decked in her full-length gown with puff sleeves.

It makes her cringe to live dirt-bound with moles,
toads, and beetles—besides she hates cold weather.

Thumbelina takes a chance on E-harmony. It's
not that she's mean, merely very picky.

Marlene at E's office suggests many a suitor.
However, at that point T believes all is a loss.

Her friend, a kind swallow, sweeps her aloft
and carries her flower-ward. She weds a small prince.

Ah, someone her size, who lives in clean meadows,
provides a real treehouse with wraparound porch.

They travel from flower to flower in flight but
damn, they had not discussed money, kids, or sex.

She recalls the bluebird who called her Maia,
he'd been always there, loving her from afar.

She could have welcomed that avian Cyrano,
and unbridled lovemaking in his large velvet nest.

Pushing up Sod

—after HBO's TV series "Six Feet Under"

Oh, Ruth, how you carry the burden of time,
a reminder of females through the ages.

You dutifully stay to take care of business,
Your husband is dead, your sons will do fine.

You are under, always under, always lower
than the dead,

watching others take rein at the podium.
Nonetheless, you are the steady oak,

the head of household around cereal bowls,
retrieving stuffed monkeys behind the stove.

How I'd love to see you shoot loud cannons.
Dance! drink! and fling your flowers.

Instead the television drones on while you
witness the ceiling drop with every hour.

Needy, needy, your red hair goes white,
your hands are clean in the midst of crimes.

I'm scared, so scared I'll shrink like you,
your small affairs aren't brash enough.

It's time for you to paint the lewd pictures,
make the big bloopers, scream with the crowd.

Push up all those caskets of time.
Rail, and turn over centuries of sod!

Beech Trees, oil on canvas, 24 x 36

Orchid

The orchid is perfect,
climbing the stake, tall
and straight, it unfolds
and arches over,
with four bright blossoms
and pale green buds that
promise to grow.
Pink petals inside white,
golden tendrils inside pink
wave—tickling the air,
awaiting company.
I arch my back on
silken sheets.
His breath is slow,
there is only endless time.
Warm fingers travel
the arch, nuzzling over
creamy hill and
strawberry nipple,
trailing downward
to softening petals below.
What once was cool melts
with a promise of lush oil.
As stem meets blossom,
tendrils tremble and yield to
sweet pain.

Chocolate Crescendos

Warm melting

dark chocolate

graham crust

crème fraiche.

Shared with a friend,

downed with cappuccino,

swirls of foamy milk.

Hey, once at the Tabard Inn with you long ago,
I had a chocolate torte which I never forgot,
and yet here I taste something better.

Perfectly moist

soothing

easy to spoon out.

Reminds me of clearing clouds that welcome sun,
late afternoon on the dock, lazy summer.
I won't go home to cook dinner.

Lie here,

sip Cointreau,

tip one more teaspoon,

soft Cadbury to my tongue.

Rocks Offshore, oil on canvas, 11 x 14

Open Air Massage at Big Sur

Afternoon rays shine low through the pampas,
hypnotized firs incline toward the waves

Shae, the masseuse, shows me the sea otters
relaxing supine, rocked gently by waves

They carry sea urchins atop their small chests,
fine feasting for them as they loll between waves

Thousands of brown bobbing knobs amid weeds are
kelp clusters, floating, pushed down by the waves

My heart beats so slowly, my legs have gone soft
The rhythm stays on right in tune with the waves

Warm shower outside, adjacent to cliffs
A flimsy breeze blows, I hear crashing waves

Sweet warmth of October before the quick night,
wrapped in hot towels, bewitched by the waves,

My fantasy heightens, I'm buoyed by the dream,
I jump to join kelp and sea otters mid waves

White Lies

I've always wondered what it's like to be promiscuous—
even though I'm not—just because I'd like to imagine it.
I've always been so curious.

Today, for example, I'll take a plane to Eleuthera,
pack a wig and some way-high heels,
Manolo Blahniks, fuchsia.

Travel First Class and order champagne, foie gras,
fromages assortis, and bite into certain dark
chocolates, throw the other halves away.

So glad I am solo, such divine rebellion—
no one knows me here. I can go topless, wear
a toe ring, even change my name.

Once on the beach, no hurry. A ceramic artist appears,
seductive smile. We'll roll on the dunes,
no mention of families.

The Path to Waterford Beach, oil on canvas, 11 x 14

Secrets I Tell Myself

When I was ten,
my friend Stephanie and I tore ends from a foam pillow
to make breasts we did not have

When I was thirteen,
I held my wrists in bed at the Honolulu Hotel
so I would not commit suicide by mistake

When I was sixteen,
I lay on the bathroom tiles feeling my stomach, my heart
thumped in my abdomen, I feared I was pregnant

When I was twenty,
I weighed 88 pounds and hid prune yogurt
in the cooler of the dance studio at college

When I was a dancer at Tanglewood,
I'm sure a famous composer
put Quaaludes in my Kool-Aid

When I was married,
I told my mother-in-law if her wonderful son
and I ever separated, we'd be good friends

When I got pregnant
by my first husband after we separated,
I told no one and insisted on abortion within a week

When I drank clear vodka for three nights
after being stalked by a schizophrenic Jesus freak
I did not tell my husband it was not water

As I am nearing seventy,
I tell myself these secrets
and repeat them to see if they are true

Seashell Symphony

Brass, strings and woodwinds take the night off—
What's a piano to do? A harp is hardly ample,
Snares and gongs on strike, tambourines have bailed.
And the house is SRO. How can a conductor cope.
Well, Seashells to the rescue showing stripes one can't imagine:
Beau's Vitronellas take the 1st Violin section, with *Dusky
Cones* as 2$^{nd\ violins}$ and *Atlantic Deer Cowries* bringing up the bass.
First movement well under way with lilting gentillesse,
the *Duskies* begin to hammer and pluck, ushering in
a fanfare of *Wentletraps*, a galore of *Ladder Horns*.
Woodwinds want their way now, *Worm Snail* clarinets caper
with a set of *Augers*, oboe-funny in their wanh-wanh.
Small purple *Turritellas* squeal, as silver piccolos are wont.
Rows and rows of *Minor Jackknifes* finger the keys,
partnered by rippling *Worm Shell Harps*.
How the robust sounds of a full-throated symphony
swell to the ceilings, cello shells doubling the slide of
the *Cabrit's Murexes*, as the tintinnabulation of triangles
and big brass roar of the *Lightning Whelks* climax to the deep
drum roll of timpanic *Oyster Shells*.
Thunderous rattling applause. You could only call it Oceanic.

Gulls Flying into the Wind, oil on canvas board, 9 x 12

Laila's Brain

Robert and Laila, my neighbors next door, so prim—
he spoke, she nodded.

Short as Napoleon, he translated at Voice of America,
she obeyed at home.

Politely, she planted while he watered flower boxes
circling the balcony.

Neighbors gathered for tea, where he held court,
Laila served banana bread, which did not rise.

At my Valentine party, when asked about first loves,
she blushed, yes,

even sparkled for a second, brown eyes dancing
below a crown of black curls.

In graceful script, she wrote a name, Peter,
something about a handsome brother—

Robert's lips turned inside out, a cat smile,
two tiger incisors flashing.

Once, collecting mail in the lobby, she whispered,
"In-laws from West Virginia arriving Friday."

By Sunday, the last terse good-byes traveled
down the corridor, Robert trailing.

A terrifying fight at 3 AM—I pressed my ear
to the door. Booming threats, withering wails

bruised the walls. Cringing, I heard whimpers
then, silence.

The following day, nothing was mentioned—
smiling, they drove to the beach.

The next time I saw them, he pushed
the wheelchair, her head, drooping,

swaddled in white cottons, one eye vacant.
He mumbled something about a crash going

over the bridge to Rehoboth. Once so self-
assured, he turned his head away.

Robert died suddenly, and Laila is alone—
head bald on top now, she does not speak.

She shuffles, uneven gait, along the balcony,
inspecting boxes of begonias.

Slouching down onto a deck chair, she rises
and sits, rises and sits, rises and

seizes her phone, forehead furrowed,
gesturing wildly—no whimpers—

Laila rages, flailing at Robert,
but no one is on the line.

Adrenaline Dog

I heard a dog bark in my dream, I've heard it many times

> Scuba test unduly cold,
> needle on my tank near zero.
> Murky quarry sucked me down,
> breath went short, rough, raspy.

Again, the warning howl

> Toaster spouting furious flames,
> growing stench of acrid smoke.
> Yanked the plug to stop the blaze,
> sirens shrieked straight to my door.

Still, another menacing snarl

> Ski tow lifted me too high,
> someone saw me hit the rail.
> A quick reflex, he cut the switch,
> adrenaline spurted in my wrists.

Mad dog growls, I clutch and swerve

> Road top strewn with angry nails,
> trucks bear down in every lane.
> Barking pulsed down through my palms
> and pulled my car to safety.

Piteous yelp, recurring scare

> Someone creeps into the room,
> footsteps near my bed.
> Still as a rock, I dare not stir,
> slit my eyes enough to stare.

Dragon Rat Nightmare

> *—after an ancient sculpture created by believers
> to protect a Shinto shrine in* Kyoto

Metal rats with rigid horns,
        steely strong with spiky scales,

scrape the ground as they drive forth,
        overtaking onyx night.

Clawing towards five human captives,
        bloody throats hurl curdling cries.

Victims stiffen, pupils dilate,
        rats' breath sears their bony shins.

Sacrificial lambs turn backwards,
        avert their faces, expose thin ankles.

Sharpened talons pierce their calves,
        barbed teeth grind Achilles heels.

Oak Leaves, oil on canvas, 11 x 14

Wretched

—inspired by Carlo Collodi's fairy tale "Pinocchio"

Geppetto throws up his hands.
The Boy has broken his heart—lies, cheats,
refuses to work, is rude in public,

and his nose gets red when he's nervous.

The Boy is equally peeved.
Geppetto has chiseled, cajoled, pleaded,
made him an anxious wreck.

Pinocchio wishes he were never conceived.

Only Cat and Fox can end it.
They seize the Boy, bind him and
sling a noose over the branch.

The Boy touches his nose, shudders, drops.
No witnesses, no tears—
both Father and Son, liberated.

That Sweet Dirty Smell of Children

Let's face it,
they're not always powder soft and edible

They smell

The sickening dried-blood whiff of scabs,
the nose-turning poop of mustard-green

Kids sniffle

The hard-sticky raspberry jam glued between braids,
the orange-brown crusted ears and noses

Really,

if only they could be hosed down with a soaking shower,
toweled,

hung to dry. Clean striped shirts,
filled with bodiless air as the wind blows

A Child Asks

What is God?

I think, not darkly,
God is death.

If ashes are ashes
and dust is dust,

I go underground and rest.
There I am fertilized

by loam and water,
beckoned by life-to-be.

When ready, I push up and
bloom color,

never knowing the hue.
I answer

the child who instinctively
knows azure is azure,

scarlet is scarlet, and
God is in the flower.

Rhododendrons and Weigelia in June, oil on canvas, 12 x 16

Yellow into Yellow

I'm several Pantone colors, though many hues confuse
and yellow has a mixed reputation

        cheerful/attentive
or
        cowardly/deceitful?

My wavelengths are the longest,
I have magnetic power. Come yellow into yellow:

Moments of pale yellow, loosely knotted skeins of yarn,
coils of friendliness, freshness of beginnings

At times, I am darker, a warning to be careful:

        Diamond-shaped danger signs
        Boxes of poison
        Beam of the flashlight

Walk with me beyond caution to read the signs:

        Don't cross the police tape
        Don't slip and fall—Piso Mojado
        Don't accelerate in the crosswalk

Dive in with me, you'll take big risks:

        If I am yellow, I am fertile
        We could birth a fable
        Color of sunshine, we could bring joy

Among Pantone colors, I'm hidden in full sight
Sometimes I arrive at places I don't know I'm going, yet

Yellow. I speak yellow:
        I can love my open passion
        I can be the clearest truth

Rebirth on the Metro Quay

I have gone and come back to life two times
in full color

Here's how:

Knife sliced my thumb,
viscous red

Tetanus shot, pure gunpowder,
blinding black. I faint once more

Now this:

Metro roars, train windows slant,
stations slip by, light dims. Cold sweat
trembles down my chest

I fight not to fade, go
blank, as rising warmth
mounts my spine

And then it's done

A woman sees me droop,
yanks me toward the door

Gray cement bench. Purse here with me.
What I took to be disappearing
comes back clear, cool

Neon-aproned station master leaning down,
"Did you eat breakfast?"

Back at work, I drink mango juice,
remove my multicolored scarf

Relief—indigo, amethyst, cyan
seep pigment anew

Reconsidering the Moon

We think you continue to change, but oceans know better.
Moon, you keep your same face towards us, a constant truth.

At *new*, we are close to each other, nocturnal animals
scamper to the shadows, badgers mate—

Your waxing crescent, a lemon slice, sneaks a peek,
waiting for the *first quarter* to test appearances.

At *full*, Australian corals release massive eggs and sperm,
doodlebugs make bigger traps for active prey.

You hide nothing, proud to show your bruises and welts.
Ungainly as you go *gibbous*, losing faith,

losing confidence, aware that the *third quarter* will
offer a stillness, time for stable reflection.

Waning crescent sweeps away all regrets, while lions attack
and kill. Scorpions grow blue in your moonlight.

Forsythia and Robins, oil on canvas board, 9 x 12

Sorrow

Loud bumps outside my apartment window—
a common city pigeon returns repeatedly.

Twigs, straw, leaves take shape of a saucer,
dotted with downy feathers from her underbelly.

What's to admire about this creature
compared to other birds? Plain. Dull.

Master craftswoman, she wedges the nest
close to the frame. A touch of iridescence

ripples slightly as she eases down
to incubate one egg. Arresting. Pretty.

Zealous mother keeps guard as juveniles
plunge and dive around wind currents.

Relieved when they leave at night, she settles,
cooing her low rumble. Window rattles.

Eighteenth day, knowing the squab may hatch,
she sets forth in the morning to feed herself.

Dignified. Regal. She will be strong,
she will protect, regardless.

The raucous adolescents cackle brashly,
loop and chase each other in the courtyard.

Careless wings slam the window, dislodge
the nest—a steep fall.

Unknowing, she retraces her path to touch down.
Which window? She makes repeated landings,

red claws clinging to the frame. Her head jerks,
bobbing. Broken choking coos.

A wracked beauty slumps against the pane.
Unforgettable.

The row of rogues, greyish pink throats,
sit silently on the adjacent roof, heads cocked.

A Life Unravels with the Day

—after Chelsea Welsh's photo series
"caught in the days unraveling"

A paisley wrap
thrown on a chair,
a burdened hairbrush
cast off there.

Auburn tresses
drown the bristles,
a dolphin rides
the purple handle.

Fair cousin Claire,
her hair grows thin,
she pulls the clumps,
shedding begins.

Her boudoir somber,
door ajar
a playful household
now macabre.

The cat slinks past,
the shades part drawn,
a mirror hanging,
upholstery worn.

Shadows echo,
pots tip over,
rugs at angles,
orange, ochre.

Paint drips downward,
birds crouch low,
vines descending,

shutters groan.
A barren life
her scalp will know,
when all is lost,
the cancer slow.

In Which I Consider Myself A Possible Woman of Algiers

> —*after Eugene Delacroix's painting*, "The Women of Algiers in their Apartment," Louvre, Paris 1834

Delacroix, like me, is charmed but deluded,
fascinated by their harem allure—
luscious flesh, bejeweled bodices,
vibrant costumes, figs.

Entering through swinging saloon doors,
I pose for them.
My magenta bloomers are brighter than theirs,
my cheeks burn violet energy.

They do not look my way,
I am disturbing the languor, familiar stupor.
Leaning on thick rugs, bolstered pillows,
these plump doyennes are adorned

with gold necklaces that sparkle against
nude chests, coyly covered by see-
through muslin blouses.
Turkish turned-up sandals,

thrown to the side, reveal
meaty feet, pudgy toes.
At times, our ladies shift positions
to ease a hip or elbow—discomfort

does not suit them.
Bored with the hookah,
they compare the men
they bedded last night:

a corpulent prince with lacquered hair;
sanctimonious merchant, smelling of musk;
odoriferous suitor, stale wine, spunk.

Spiritless, they wait uncounted hours,
tomorrow night will be a repeat.
Blue-black Algerian servant,
Samia, turns away from them,
she's heard it all before.

The mirror on the tiled wall above them
tilts forward, she has not bothered
to straighten it.

She stops abruptly when she sees me.
Am I a new consort?
She determines not,
we are kindred spirits she and I,

different kinds of gems.
We recognize this luxuriant space as dark,
light shines through a depressed window
but to no end.

It doesn't go anywhere,
only opens to the kitchen
where Samia is headed.
I believe it leads to Exodus,

we could run fast,
holding hands to escape this confinement.
As I attempt to find my way
across the circle of ladies,
a putrid smell rises—

moths in the drapes, cockroaches
in the corner, truth exhaling
from the rotten flesh of women
under those bloomers.

Dressed-up dolls dulled by men
who tell them they are well-taken care of,
they don't realize their pearl anklets,
endless hashish, servants-in-waiting keep them

captive for life.
I pick my way through an airless world
across plush carpets to follow brave Samia.
At least, Delacroix had foresight to render her

with fleet feet and shoes on.

Blossoms by Fishers Island Sound, oil on canvas, 8 x 10

The Underside of Color

—after Marc Chagall's "Paris Through the Window,"
Guggenheim Museum, NYC 1913

Chagall invites me to his house—he knows I love this painting

He leaves the front door open, I arrive early. Seated on the right side of the parlor, locket in my palm, I wait

Chenille, nervous cat, emerald green tail, sits on the sill listening. Shouts from the street are loud, one side of the window is open

Aromatic warm baguettes, clinking cups from the café below. Colors roar across the sky

Swaths of vermillion, streaks of royal blue, icy white shafts illuminate the sky, turning the Eiffel Tower shimmering white

The spire shares light with rows of dollhouse-size dwellings
and wraps a beam around the right side of my head

Et voilà! We're startled by the oncoming whoosh of Chagall's parachute rushing toward us, plummeting down toward his floral-back chair. He lands, offers absinthe

He's happy, he's sad. He had a vision of his parents descending—
miniature black horizontal figures floating head to head,
bickering in joyful Yiddish

They stay with him everywhere, wave as he passes. They know how he loves Paris, beautiful Bella, why he paints his fish, fancy fiddlers, harlequin clowns

Behind buoyant colors, someone is saying Kaddish. Sadness seeps from the city smoke stacks. We sip, melding into lament

Chenille jumps down, slinks to the kitchen, sniffing for herring. She knows
Chagall adores her, comes back to rub her neck up his trouser leg

He's laughing, he's sobbing. Fantasy and gravity counter-balance.
My two heads, two hearts weep with love and contradiction.

Story Tower

    —inspired by Nikolai Rimsky-Korsakov's "Scheherazade,"
    the music and the story

Building story on story
Balcony by balcony
Windows through blinds—

        We frame our lives

Your oboe takes us forward,
We heed recurring themes
A river flows unwinding

        with currents underneath

The leavings too familiar,
Arpeggios gone rogue
Each day a chapter lengthens,

        each year the epic grows

We deflect, we hide in labor,
Your trumpets push us on
We raise the shades of mourning,

        a seed becomes a rose

We soften as your harps wrap
Around the violins
Torment melts to forgiveness

        reprise becomes reprieve

There's a rhythm to our days now,
Remorse and anguish end
We know this lilting story

        we climb the stairs again

We need one thousand stories,
To fall in love so slowly
A tender piccolo's refrain—

                    standing on balconies, I remain

What to Expect at Congressional Cemetery

Not the graves that drew me there,
not the closed iron gates where I found an opening,
not the numbered maps leading to celebrity markers—

I tuned to the un named, the no ones, the un knowns.

Confused by the totem poles along the brick walk,
distracted by the verse I was waiting for,
bewildered by grief and loss and heat—

I blinked through sweat, pulled my straw hat low.

Amused by the K-9 dog-walkers
who paid to be in the special society of cemetery donors,
we all were deciphering Washington DC anew.

Not the St Albans where my first husband taught,
not the Van Ness building where I lived for 28 years,
not the Eastern Market flat I rented during separation—

I tuned to hundred years of burying:

The 1892 epitaphs from husband to wives,
tipped-back headstones of proud gay lovers,
locked vaults built by self-claimed venerables made

me flee back to the totems, the red carved cedars—

Female bear of liberty,
male eagle of war,
turtle in the middle of the crossbar.

I learned comfort from carver Jewel Praying Wolf James
from Lummi Nation, a Washington far from Washington.
This is the verse I was waiting for, the distraction

I sought: All our arms are linked underground
wrapped around one another. All our crooked
feet know pain and suffering.

Mother Earth holding us up,
Father Sun covering us down,
dogs and their keepers walking across our kidney stones.

Longings

Lovers talk and walk
along hedges neatly carved.
A man sits alone,
on a plain wooden platform,
watching koi glide silently.

Among the bonsai,
old wise voices seem to cry.
Haunting serenades,
protests for the lonely one.
Low moans for full lungs of air.

View from the Branford Hospice, oil on canvas, 11 x 14

Cento: The Self, The Soul, The Body

—after Sylvia Plath, William Carlos Williams, John Ashbery, Gerard Manley Hopkins, Elizabeth Bishop, William B. Yeats, Stephen Dunn, and Sharon Olds

Standing on their shoulders, I listen to all the voices chant

I am the arrow…

In a case like this, I know quick action is the main thing.

I don't understand myself, only segments of myself that misunderstand each other—

(I sit) *on meadow and river and wind-wandering and weed-winding bank,*

one foot of the sun steadies itself,

(and) *as I cast out remorse,*

so great a sweetness flows into the breast

we must laugh, and we must sing.

No one should ask the other, "What were you thinking?"

I lie there in the air as if flying rapidly without moving, and slowly I cool off.

Strange Currency

If I could buy a sunset,
        I'd be rich in your scent—
a dusting of salt and black opium.

If I could purchase the memory,
        I'd wrap it in featherweight
lace to keep it almost intangible.

If I could retain the passion, I'd
        think of the moment I
blurted I love you and you responded.

Ever rich—I'd swim in the
        tenderness of amplified
feeling, up-breaths of excitement—

I'd replay the evening on the beach,
        your palms grazing my ribs,
smoothing down my hips.

For this, I'd pay a gazillion starfish
        and pocketsful of
doubloons that chime.

Mindscapes

Tightly buckled in my seat
I spy that oval window—

Heaps of quilted clouds below
beckon me to venture.

There was a time I would not jump,
now my gut has muscle.

Disregarding facts that frown,
and reasons to stay cabin-bound,

I catch sweet currents as I dive,
glancing down on spongey-grey,

plunging onto foamy mounts
that billow up and send me out.

I smell clean ice in gauzy wisps,
gentle crystals pass me by,

I taste the fresh of water pure,
the swallowing is easy.

There are no laws of physics here,
I reach these bracing peaks at will.

Streaming over clouds I'm on,
I have the lift of papillons.

Looking back to plane-bound times,
where earthly reason kept me still,

I know that I must leap to reach
the untapped landscapes of my mind.

Looking Upriver at Riverrun, oil on canvas

Acknowledgments

My great appreciation to Donna Baier Stein, Editor, and Lisa Sawyer, Managing Editor, of *Tiferet Journal*, where poems in this book, sometimes in earlier versions, first appeared:

"Adrenaline Dog"
"My Dinner with Athena"
"Victorian Ghost"

To Annemarie Lockhart, Founding Editor, and Nathan Gunter, Managing Editor, of *vox poetica* for publishing:

"Reconsidering the Moon"
"Sorrow"

To Karen Lyon, Literary Editor of *The Hill Rag*, for publishing:

"What to Expect at Congressional Cemetery"

And to Lorette Luzajic, Editor and Founder of *The Ekphrastic Review*, for publishing:

"In Which I Consider Myself A Possible Woman of Algiers"
"Story Tower"
"The Underside of Color"

Thanks

I am grateful to the people who made this book possible:

my sister and first reader, novelist Betsy Woodman, my writing guru and co-conspirator since she was six and I was four

the magical visionaries at *The Writer's Hotel* and *The New Guard Review*: Founding Editor, Shanna McNair, and Consulting Editor, Scott Wolven

my cherished friends and writing companions, Sarah Toth and Bill Kircher, who read many versions of these poems with me

my extraordinary critics and master poets: Grace Cavalieri, Chris Bursk, Sue Ellen Thompson, Richard Blanco, and Alexandra Oliver

my steadfast supporters: Susan Clampitt, Jeremy Waletzky, Virginia Rice, Stephanie Cotsirilos, and Tanner Stening

my generous instructors from The Writer's Center in Bethesda, Maryland: Judith Harris, Meg Eden, Nan Fry, and Alexis Pope, and from *Sun Magazine*'s annual conference, "Into the Fire": Heather Sellers, Joe Wilkins, and Sparrow

List of Paintings

Daffodils & Small Waterfall 3

Nehantic Park 7

Looking Down Into North Adams, ... 10

Beech-Trees 13

Rocks Offshore 16

The Path to Waterford Beach 19

Gulls Flying Into the Wind 22

Oak Leaves 27

Rhododendrons and Weigelai in June 31

Forsythia & Robins Charles 35

Blossoms by Fishers Island Sound 43

View from the Branford Hospice 51

Looking Upriver at Riverun 55

About the Art

By Richard Harteis

Purists in the world of poetry find it anathema to combine the visual arts with the verbal, but it has been our belief that including two artists in different fields only enhances the work of each, and is an additional pleasure for a reader. The paintings by Charles Reyburn in this collection are not meant to "illustrate" the poems by Lee Woodman, though at times there is a synchronicity of themes. Both artists have created visions of the world – one with paint, the other with verbal images, and often the dreamlike quality of the poems matches quite beautifully the impressionist vision Charles Reyburn offers us. Several of Lee's poems are ekphrastic : a response to a work of art through poetry. Perhaps we'll see such a poem soon on a painting by Charles Reyburn.

I first got to know Charles Reyburn several years ago when he came to do paintings of Riverrun, William Meredith's home on the Thames which was designated an historic landmark in the State of Connecticut in 2008. Since our first meeting, Charles has continued to exhibit his work; and, his very beautiful impressionist sketches are becoming well known in Southeastern Connecticut and beyond. He is really a lovely guy, recently married to Trish Reyburn, true Nutmeggers both with extended families and friends here the area. We're so pleased that he has generously offered us his work to share with readers and we congratulate him on a wonderful career.

About the Author

Lee Woodman's love of language and the arts began in her childhood years in India and France. An internationally recognized media producer, her radio and film awards include five CINEs, two NY International Film Blue Ribbons, and three Gracies from American Women in Radio and Television. She worked for 20 years in leadership roles at the Smithsonian, was Vice-President of Media and Editorial at K12, Inc., and Executive Producer at Lee Woodman Media, Inc. Her clients included The Library of Congress, The World Bank, Public Radio International, NPR, and the Fulbright Program.

Lee's essays and poems have appeared in *Tiferet Journal, Zócalo Public Square, Grey Sparrow Press, The Ekphrastic Review, vox poetica, The New Guard Review, The Concord Monitor,* and forthcoming in *Naugatuck River Review*. Her first poetry collection, HOMESCAPES, explored her memories from the far reaches of the globe to a family cabin in New Hampshire. A Pushcart nominee, she has received two Individual Poetry Fellowships from the DC Commission on the Arts and Humanities.

Lee lives in Washington, DC.

Artist Statement

By Lee Woodman:

Choreographing words is my passion. I write to turn sound and images into emotion and story, and to share with others the surprising landscapes of the mind. Poems are the way I explore joy and sorrow, longing, fear, and rage. I choose varied poetic forms from traditional to contemporary—pantoum, villanelle, free verse and narrative—to fit and enhance content. Adding scents, tastes, and textures, I revel in nature and struggle to understand the territory of the heart. Who are some characters in the MINDSCAPES collection? Greek goddesses, ghosts, orchids, scorpions, and seashells. They help clarify difficult life decisions, blend fantasy and reality, and open worlds as only poetry can.

www.ingramcontent.com/pod-product-compliance
Lightning Source LLC
Chambersburg PA
CBHW042120100526
44587CB00025B/4134